REPTILE OR AMPHIBIAN?

by Laura Crawford

PEARSON
Scott
Foresman

DK

What You Already Know

All living things, or organisms, are made up of cells. A cell is the smallest unit of life. Each cell consists of many parts. At the center of a cell is the nucleus, which controls the cell's activity. The cytoplasm has everything the cell needs to carry out life processes. Plant cells have chloroplasts that trap energy from the Sun to make food.

Plants and animals are classified into groups called kingdoms. Kingdoms are divided into smaller groups. These smaller groups provide the scientific names for organisms. The first part of an organism's scientific name is its genus. The second part is its species. The animal kingdom consists of two main groups. Vertebrates are animals with backbones. Invertebrates are animals without backbones.

animal cell

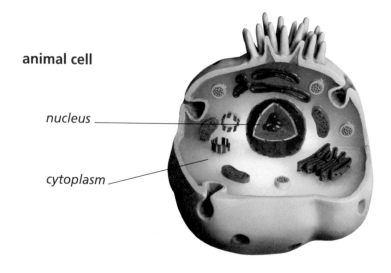

nucleus

cytoplasm

In the plant kingdom, vascular plants transport water and nutrients through vascular tissue. Nonvascular plants, however, pass water and nutrients from one cell to the next. Some plants reproduce with flowers or cones that produce seeds. Other plants reproduce with spores.

Animals have adaptations that allow them to survive in their environment. Some animals are adapted to blend into their environment. Animals have instincts, such as migration and hibernation, to help them survive. Animals also inherit and learn behavior from their parents.

The animal kingdom is very large and has many different groups. Two of these groups are reptiles and amphibians.

The crocodile is a reptile.

Introduction

Reptiles and amphibians are two animal groups that are often confused. They have many things in common. Both groups are cold-blooded vertebrates. Most of them hatch from eggs. But reptiles and amphibians also have important differences.

More than 3,140 species of amphibians live on Earth today. They range in length from 1 centimeter to 1.5 meters. Frogs and toads, with approximately 2,660 different species, make up the largest group of amphibians. They have powerful hind legs, which make them good jumpers. The next largest group, the salamanders, has around 320 species. Salamanders can be identified by their long tails. The smallest group of amphibians is the caecilians (suh-SIL-yuhnz). There are only about 160 caecilian species. These legless amphibians are sometimes confused with earthworms or snakes, but they are very different from both.

The European fire salamander is an amphibian.

The tegu lizard is a reptile.

There are approximately 6,000 species of reptiles on Earth today. More than 3,000 of the species are lizards, the largest group of reptiles. Snakes make up the second largest reptile group. There are more than 2,500 species of snakes. Turtles and tortoises are next, with approximately 250 species. There are more than 20 species of crocodilians, including alligators and crocodiles. There is only one species of a very rare beaked reptile called a tuatara (too-uh-TAH-ruh).

Like amphibians, reptiles vary greatly in size. Some snakes and lizards are as small as 5 centimeters. But some crocodiles and snakes grow more than 12 meters long!

The study of reptiles and amphibians is called herpetology. This word comes from the word *herpeton*, which means "crawling things."

Caecilian

Amphibians

Amphibians live all over the world. They can live in water or on land. Since most amphibians have skin that must be kept moist, they usually live near water.

Frogs and toads can be found in every climate except polar regions and very dry deserts. Caecilians often burrow in the loose soil of tropical forests. They also live in rivers and streams. Salamanders live in ponds, swamps, wet mountain forests, and grasslands.

Frogs have large eyes that allow them to see in many directions.

The head and tail of a caecilian are hard to tell apart.

Salamanders are amphibians that keep their tails as adults.

Reptiles

Reptiles can be found in just about any habitat except polar regions and tundras. Many reptiles have scaly skin, which holds in water and prevents their bodies from drying out.

Crocodiles and alligators tend to live near water. Turtles also live near water, while tortoises prefer dry land. Lizards and snakes make their homes on the ground or in trees. Tuataras often burrow.

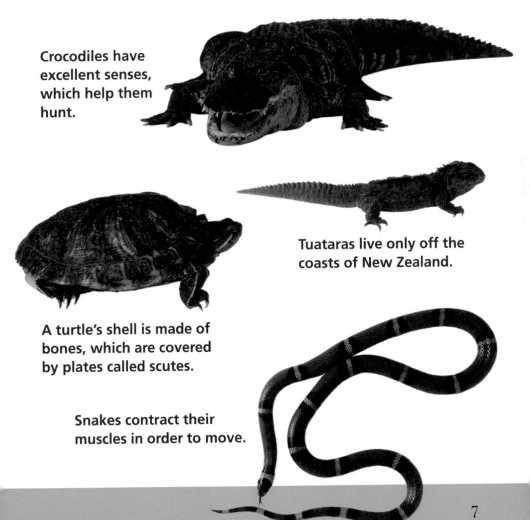

Crocodiles have excellent senses, which help them hunt.

Tuataras live only off the coasts of New Zealand.

A turtle's shell is made of bones, which are covered by plates called scutes.

Snakes contract their muscles in order to move.

Skin and Structure

Although all reptiles and amphibians are vertebrates, the number of vertebrae, or bony segments, they have varies greatly. Some snakes have as many as 400 vertebrae. But their jaws are what makes them different from amphibians and other reptiles. Some snakes are able to open their jaws wide enough to swallow their prey whole. The two halves of the lower jaw are connected by muscle and ligaments, rather than by bone. Snakes can swallow a huge chunk of food all at once, allowing them to go long periods of time without eating.

The spine of a frog or toad usually has fewer than 12 vertebrae. Spines of salamanders have between 30 and 100 vertebrae while spines of caecilians can have more than 200.

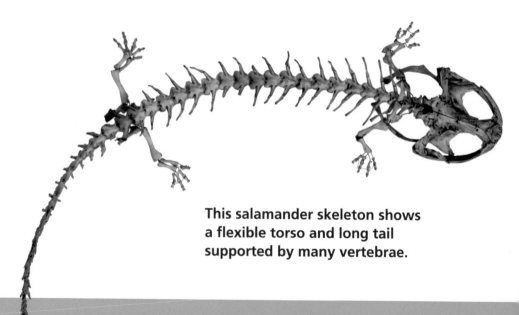

This salamander skeleton shows a flexible torso and long tail supported by many vertebrae.

Amphibians and reptiles are cold-blooded creatures, or ectotherms. They depend on the environment to regulate their body temperature. Some are warmed directly by the Sun. Others regulate their body temperature by staying on warm surfaces. Most reptiles and amphibians become dormant when it gets too cold. Some amphibians living in colder climates hibernate. Tuataras are the only reptiles that can stay active in colder temperatures. They have been known to survive in temperatures as low as 6°C (43°F) due to their slow heart rate and breathing.

White's tree frog has shiny, waxlike skin.

Amphibians have soft, smooth skin that is water permeable. This means that water can enter their bodies through their skin. Reptiles are covered in rough, dry skin that does not let water into their bodies. The skin of a snake does not grow with it. So snakes periodically shed their skin. This is called molting.

Notice the scales on this Madagascan day gecko.

Land or Water?

The word amphibian comes from the Greek word *amphibios*, which means "a being with a double life." Most young amphibians live in water. As they get older, they live both on land and in water. Some spend their entire lives moving between land and water.

Amphibians need water to keep their skin moist. Water passes through an amphibian's skin into its body. Amphibians might take in some water with food or gather it from wet surfaces, but they rarely drink it. They also need water when laying eggs.

The palmate newt is a kind of salamander. The webbing between its back toes helps it swim rapidly.

The mangrove snake spends most of its time looking for prey in the trees of Malaysia and other parts of Asia.

Unlike many amphibians, not all reptiles need to be close to water. Some reptiles, such as lizards, live in the desert.

Snakes live in many habitats around the world, both where water is plentiful and where it is hard to find. A few species of snakes are found on islands or in places that have cold winters.

Alligators and crocodiles live in large bodies of water where they swim and hunt for food. Crocodiles can also be found on land.

This alligator is crawling into the water, where it will wait for unsuspecting prey.

Legs and Feet

The legs and feet of reptiles differ from species to species. The basilisk is a lizard with long, thin toes on each foot. When frightened, it rears up on its hind legs and runs quickly across both land and water.

Sea turtles are strong swimmers. Their front limbs are shaped like paddles. These paddles help them move successfully in water, but they make walking on land difficult and awkward.

Small lizards called climbing geckos are equipped with pads on each of their toes. These pads are covered with thousands of thin, hairlike projections called setae (SEE-tee). The setae cling to any surface they touch, enabling the geckos to stick to the surface as well.

The huge front legs of this sea turtle act like paddles.

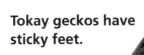

Tokay geckos have sticky feet.

The structure of amphibians' limbs also varies from species to species. When toads and frogs hatch, they do not have legs. As they change and develop, they grow legs that help them live on land.

Frogs and toads are able to hop due to their long and powerful hind legs. When they jump, they first push off the ground with their front legs and arch their back so they are facing upwards. Then they push with their hind legs, sending them flying into the air!

Like climbing geckos, tree frogs have pads on their toes. These pads allow the frogs to climb on different surfaces, including trees.

Most salamanders are hatched with legs, but their legs never develop to be very strong. They walk slowly in a diagonal path. Some salamanders, called sirens, live mostly in the water. These salamanders have no hind legs and very small front legs. They move by waving their tail back and forth like an eel.

A duck-billed tree frog grasps a tree with its strong legs.

Self-Defense

Amphibians and reptiles have different ways to protect themselves. Hiding is the most common form of defense. Snakes and lizards often hide in bushes, while crocodiles, turtles, and frogs may go underwater.

Some reptiles and amphibians have more advanced ways of hiding. Many lizards, such as skinks and chameleons, use camouflage to blend in with their surroundings. Camouflage can be anything that makes it difficult for other animals to find them. Chameleons even have the ability to change the color of their skin so that they can hide in many different places.

Mimicry is when an animal's body resembles something else in nature so that the animal is better able to survive. A leaf-tailed gecko's brown body looks very similar to the leaves in which it hides.

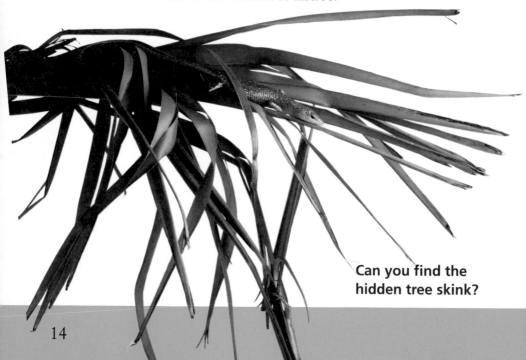

Can you find the hidden tree skink?

This newt larva will live in the water until it becomes an adult.

Some reptiles lay eggs, while others give birth to their offspring. Reptile eggs have a hard or leathery shell. This helps keep moisture in. The eggs do not need to be laid in water. Unlike amphibians, reptiles look like their parents when they are born.

Reptile parents protect their eggs to varying degrees. Some lizards return to the nest to turn their eggs. Some female pythons stay with their eggs until they hatch. However, most reptiles leave soon after they lay their eggs.

Snakes can either give birth to live young, or they can lay eggs. In either case, when the young are born, they are independent and able to take care of themselves. They do not need very much help from their parents.

A snake emerges from its egg.

Frog Reproduction

Frogs lay eggs that mature outside of the adults' bodies. When frogs produce eggs, it is called spawning. Soon the tiny fertilized eggs become tadpoles. Tadpoles use gills to get oxygen. They have a tail to help them swim. As the tadpoles get older, they begin to grow lungs and legs. Their eyes move to a new position, and they lose their tail. Adults frogs don't need a tail to help them swim because they spend most of their time on land.

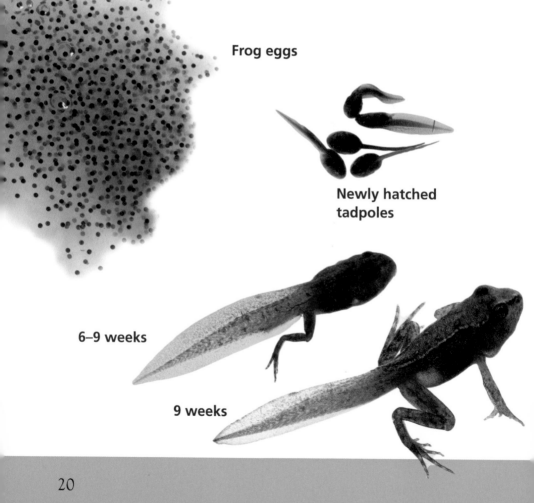

Frog eggs

Newly hatched tadpoles

6–9 weeks

9 weeks

Tortoise Reproduction

Tortoises are turtles that live on land. Before a female leopard tortoise lays her eggs, she digs a large hole with her hind feet. She later drops groups of five to thirty white eggs, called a clutch, into the hole. She then covers the eggs with dirt. Baby tortoises will hatch from their shells anywhere from six months to more than a year later.

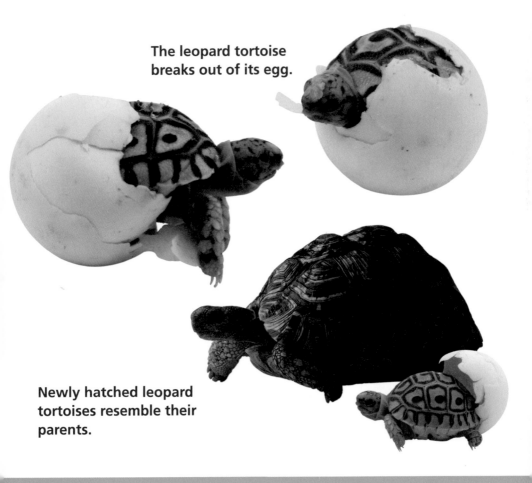

The leopard tortoise breaks out of its egg.

Newly hatched leopard tortoises resemble their parents.

Similar but Different

There are similarities between reptiles and amphibians that cause confusion. Reptiles and amphibians are both cold-blooded vertebrates. Both reptiles and amphibians use their senses, such as smell and sight, to find food and stay away from predators. But when you compare the two kinds of animals, you will notice important differences. Amphibians have moist skin without scales. Most amphibians must live near water so their soft skin does not dry out. Reptiles have dry, scaly skin. Their skin does not need as much water as the skin of amphibians does, so they do not always live near water.

Different species of reptiles have different types of legs and feet. Some species, such as snakes, have no legs or feet at all! Most amphibians hatch as larvae, many of which do not have arms or legs. Many will grow limbs when they undergo metamorphosis.

chameleon

Many amphibians and reptiles can hide from enemies because their skin blends into their environment. Some reptiles can even change the color of their skin to make it more difficult for predators to find them. Other species have poisons that give them added protection from predators.

paradoxical frog

Most amphibians reproduce by laying soft eggs in the water. Reptiles either lay eggs that have a protective shell, or they give birth to their young.

Scientists have classified thousands of species of reptiles and amphibians. The two groups of animals have many similarities. They also have many differences. Sometimes even animals in the same group seem quite different. Snakes and turtles don't look much alike, but they are both reptiles. The worm-like caecilians look nothing like frogs, but both are amphibians. Scientists study the two groups to learn more about the relationships, adaptations, and behavior that have helped the animals survive.

corn snake

Glossary

burrow   to dig a hole or tunnel in the ground

clutch   a group of animal eggs

ectotherm   a cold-blooded animal

herpetology   the study of reptiles and amphibians

mimicry   an animal's resemblance to something in nature, which helps the animal to hide

molting   the periodic shedding of an outer covering, such as skin

setae   hairlike projections on the pads of a gecko's feet